HOW TO MAKE LOVE LAST

Blanshard & Blanshard

PAGE ADDIE PRESS
GREAT BRITAIN. AUSTRALIA

KEEP
THE SEX
DIRTY
&
THE FIGHTS
CLEAN

This book is first class; Keep the Sex Dirty and the Fights Clean is crammed from beginning to end with excellent advice on how to get the most from your relationship. A five star read for sure. The genius of Blanshard & Blanshard is their ability to drill right down into the relationship aspects that matter most to both ourselves and our partners and then to guide us gently to the appropriate solution. Blanshard and Blanshard understand that we need to understand our partners and cherish our relationships and that therein lies the key to a fulfilling and adventurous sex life.

Redwel

I would recommend this book to anyone who wants to learn more about their partner, about themselves, have better sex and generally improve their relationship.

Keep The Sex Dirty and the Fights Clean touches on all topics that come with being in a relationship and that includes sex. I would suggest reading the sections about sex. They are very insightful! I also particularly enjoyed all the sections on arguing and fighting. If you are in a long-term relationship then chances are you will argue with your partner now and then. After reading this book I now understand that there is a "how" to arguing in a relationship that is more affective for communication and less damaging.

Andy (Spain)

I thought a self-help book about relationships would be the standard dull step-by-step facts that are a chore to read. Wow, is this anything but! This was a very fun and informative read. Blanshard and Blanshard really know relationships. And they make reading the less saucy information more fun. Perhaps like medicine coated in chocolate flavored Viagra. Filled with great tips to argue less and really enjoy your relationship in a meaningful loving and exciting way. "Keep the Sex Dirty and the Fights Clean" delves deeper into relationships with great information that made me say out loud, "I didn't know that" and "ooooo, that's nice". I definitely have a few things to try with my husband now!

Mary (San Fransisco)

Keep the sex dirty and the fights clean is a great relationship book. I have been married for almost 12 years and a lot of what I read really hit home and made me think about my relationship. This is a must read for anyone who wants to ignite the spark back in their relationship and learn something new about themselves.

R J, Brewer

CONTENTS

KEEP THE SEX DIRTY

BACK TO BASIC INSTINCTS

Sex is the premise of this book! *Blanshard & Blanshard* are back talking about relationships. This time we're hitting on a topic that is so vital to successful relationships, yet far too few people talk honestly about it. Sex.

The way we see it, there are two kinds of sex. Dirty Sex and Maintenance Sex. When we say dirty sex, we don't mean a dictionary definition of: adj: 1. grimy, soiled, spotted, stained (unless it's your gorgeous thousand thread Egyptian cotton bedsheets!) We don't mean getting down and dirty jellymud wrestling either. Because when you're in the mood, you can share a shower together and have fantastic 'dirty' sex. So what exactly is dirty sex? What *Blanshard & Blanshard* have come to figure out is this. Dirty sex is fantastic sex; the opposite of boring sex. Getting down and dirty is back to basic instincts as a couple. Whatever feels good for you and your partner qualifies. Basic bawdy, raunchy, hot, lustful, risqué, lickerish, wanton, abandoned, suggestive, tempting, steamy or blue. Leave those details up to you. Or down to you. It's a touchy feely thing. You amp up your sexual urges a thousand fold, when you say what you like and you let your partner know exactly what feels good for you. And vice versa. All for one and one for all! There's a kind of sex that leaves you with lipstick smudged and wild tousled hair. Sex which leaves a beautiful afterglow that makes people say "Hey! what have you guys been up too!"

The opposite of dirty sex is what *Blanshard & Blanshard* call Maintenance Sex. N: preservation, care, yard-work! We all know that one. Maintenance Sex is as predictable as brushing your teeth. It's worked for years. Why change a good thing, right? Wrong!

Maintenance Sex is what couples do when they slip into routine. Maintenance Sex is sex as most couples do it. Jump into bed, turn down the light, a little foreplay, or not, kiss and get down to it. Sex happens, as soft and familiar as your favourite pillow, as comfortable as your sofa, as reliable as your grandmother's recipe for chocolate cake. Perfectly o.k. and pleasurable. Yeah! But can you say it's really great sex? Or does maintenance sex involve a certain degree of compromise. A step down from how fantastic sex can be. Perhaps only one of you is feeling in the mood and the other goes along for the ride. Or you or your partner may want to make love to keep the feeling of being sexually connected. Nothing wrong with that! How you make love together is private and personal. But the more you put into your sex life the more you'll get into it. So enjoy slipping between the sheets with *Keep The Sex Dirty And The Fights Clean.*

-Blanshard & Blanshard

KEEP
THE FIGHTS CLEAN

DON'T MISS OUT
ON PLEASURES
BELOW THE BELT.

What *Blanshard & Blanshard* know is this: don't disrespect the person you love. If you verbally or emotionally attack when you argue, (instead of dealing with the issue) then you are 'Dirty Fighting.' Do that and you'll miss out on the pleasures below the belt.

Words can make or break your relationship. When you fire off your mouth with a grand slam attack on someone's character, you'll lose their trust and respect. Once you say something hurtful, you can't unsay it. Memory doesn't unravel like that.

When the fighting is dirty, you're out to wound the other person as deeply as possible. From inside love, every word that comes out of your mouth during a heated argument is a weapon. You say things that are false for the sting effect of getting back at your partner. You exaggerate to get a reaction. This is the worst kind of fighting. It's unfair fighting, it's dirty. If you're not conscious of what you say, your words can hurt your partner badly. And this leaves the other person feeling abandoned and humiliated.

When you argue take care. What is said is never forgotten. You want to be able to look back on any disagreement and not have any negative emotions. Think of words as having permanence. Choose words very thoughtfully. What you say matters. So make an effort to keep all your fights clean.

Start by defining the problem. Be as specific as you can. When two people 'define' what they want to talk about, they won't end up arguing for long and going over and over the same ground. What they talk about is clearer. Avoid general terms. If your discussions do go off track, you won't wander as far from the point, but will return to the same spot from where you started the conversation.

You can go from link to link along the chain of discussion, following each others chain of thought, until you reach the last link in the chain you'll understand the issue and see the other person's point of view.

When you respect each other, you won't end up sorting out an issue through a dirty fight scene. Or worse, having a deep nagging sense that you've gained another negative perspective about your partner and your relationship. When you keep the fights clean, you forget that style or mode of retaliation. You both understand that the task is not to fix each other, not to change what your partner thinks or believes, but to gain understanding and greater respect for each other.

Once you set the rules and agree to make an effort to understand each other rather than create unsustainable conflict, your relationship comes out on top every time. You are doing good works! And there's a tangible benefit when you keep the fights clean.

Fight in a way that's constructive and you intensify your interaction together. This is when a fight brings you closer together. When you keep the fights clean, you and your partner have fight freedom - the freedom to deal with any problem. You solve issues with focus, simply because you avoid extended bouts of emotional conflict.

When you keep the fights clean, you'll notice how you avoid the aftermath a fight causes. Less recovery time means less time trying to make up (hours, days, weeks, months, years) and more time to make-out. Even if you haven't reached a solution and are still working on it, there is a peaceful feeling when you know your fights stay clean. No nasty verbal punches. Ding! Ding! No bad feelings. Ding! Smile. You guys are o.k.

Simply being aware of how you argue and setting up new ground rules is the first step in sorting out sparring matches between you. You'll find yourself loving each others differences. The more intimacy...the greater your sex life. When relationships work like this, you and your partner are the ones who are so together, you can't help making bedroom eyes in public!

WHY DIRTY SEX ROCKS

DIRTY SEX IS NOT JUST ANY SEX.

You know the saying 'get down and dirty'. *Blanshard & Blanshard* say it's true. Dirty sex is not just any sex. Dirty sex is more than regular maintenance sex. By contrast, dirty sex is transforming and healing. Dirty sex takes more time than maintenance sex. Dirty sex is about making love as a complete sexual-sensual experience. Dirty sex connects you to each other.

Both partners share a mutual afterglow for hours and even days afterwards. All seems right in your world. Dirty sex makes you feel closer every time you make love. Any sense of separateness dissolves away in a kiss.

Couples who have great sex together feel spiritually connected as soul mates. Dirty sex is making love with honesty and trust. Letting go, coming closer together and just being your true self with your partner.

Dirty sex is making love in the most connected way possible; not holding back, but being conscious and unconscious in the moments of sharing your whole sexual being, your mind, body and soul with your partner. Dirty uninhibited sex is melting or dissolving into mutual orgasm. A deeply bonding experience of dream, touch, kiss, passion.

Every time you make love, you share intimate feelings. This helps strengthen your personal lives. You share erotic, sexy secrets. You feel the power of love. Sexual feelings are so powerful they build a bond of togetherness. And this strongly bonded feeling does not disappear. You add to it, each time you have sex. You make a deep connection through sex. As you do, you build up your relationship. Making love has a cumulative effect. The more physical love you share, the greater emotional love you feel. Deep feelings accumulate through having great sex. In fact, you will feel more in love with your partner, than when you first met.

SEXUAL ALLSORTS

MORE THAN JUST BIRTHDAY SEX.

Maintenance Sex, is general upkeep sex that easily turns into Seasonal Sex, the first fall of snow. Annual sex, Christmas, birthdays, New Year. Special sex, when you win, get a new job. Make-up Sex, the way you get back together after an argument. Then there's fight make up sex, fight maybe sex, fight goodbye sex!

The routine of sex, while safe, can lead to sex being bottom of the list of jobs to do. Now, your once passionate encounters turn into assorted sex. Quickie sex. Last minute sex. Squeeze one in sex. O.K sex. Catch up sex. If I have to sex. If you want to sex. We haven't had sex in a while kind of sex.

Often one partner complains that they are too tired to make love. And the other person has a headache. So days turn into weeks and weeks into months and before you know you are making love once a month. Life gets in the way of love. Yet, sex is critical to a great, long-lasting relationship. Sex should rate high in your love life. Neglect sex and everything eventually supersedes sex. Until one day you realize that you haven't made love for two weeks, two months, two years or longer. Notice how grumpy you both get when you don't have sex. How fights develop out of the blue often because you want to get close. But you're both untouchable!

X RATED

THE A-Z OF SEX.

Variety is spicy. To keep the sex side of your relationship raunchy and never remotely touching on boring. You need to go against the idea of maintenance sex: you take up the same positions, do it in the same place, on the same day, at the same time. All of which leaves you feeling that secretly sex is over rated, not that much fun, better things to do with your time, not worth making an effort over, something which makes you hide a yawn, lie back and think of shopping. That's how you end up bored with each other !

Understand that sex is an unlimited act of extreme pleasure. The more you put out, the more you're going to bling in the whole sex thing. After all, it's your bed, your bodies.

Fantasy, try it out. Watch a sexy movie, read a sexy book together. Check out condoms that offer more than protection. Condoms with raised bumps, ribbed ripple,

Pina Colada flavours, and some even pulsate. A hotter sex life could be discovered on the shelves of your local pharmacy. Turn on bedtime toys. Good vibrations are up to you. Talk to your partner before pulling out a play-box of adventurous things.

What turns you on individually and as a couple is strictly private. Only the walls in cheap motels have ears. Dirty sex is about losing inhibitions and just getting down and doing what feels right. Maybe all or none of the above. There is no score card, no goal keeper, no referee. What ever feels good...even what feels a little naughty or a tad taboo, may be natural for you two. What really turns you on probably qualifies. It may be all in your head. Pretending someone is watching you to get it on. Or touching in front of your partner and seeing how long they can keep their hands off you or themselves! Or go for adventurous sex, making love in an abandoned railway station, on a deserted beach, a coconut thatch shack or in a tent under the stars.

You can tell couples who have a great physical time together. It shows because outwardly they appear more together. They look at each other with interest. And when they talk it's personal and intimate. You can't help notice the couple who have an obvious, intimate connection between them. People often ask them, what their secret is. Physical attraction, passion, intimacy and a huge helping of dirty sex.

Couples who are intimate do not put their sex life on the proverbial back-burner; but they make hot sex a number one activity. They don't allow work and the outside world to dominate waking hours, leaving little time to get it on. Sure, you get busy. Your partner makes adjustments when you're working all hours. They start accepting without complaint when you say you are too tired to make love. They stop complaining and telling you they want to spend more time with you. They give up expecting you to be there. Eventually, it occurs to you to put more effort into the relationship. You plan to take a week off, only to find out that your partner has made other plans. They no longer wait till you switch off the computer, turn off the TV and feel in the mood. They adapt to the fact that you are only there, sometimes, physically or emotionally for them. But not enough to make them feel desired and sexually fulfilled as a lover. The sad part is, they adjust their emotional needs to not needing you.

You both start feeling out of touch and in the worst case scenario, estranged from each other. You end up doing more things separately and you can end up so apart as a couple, that you end up separating and going different ways. When you take your sexual connection for granted, you can lose what you have.

It is a three stage process. First, you let your sex life slip below the radar. You don't need each other as much as you used too. Then, you adjust to the lack of interest and lose interest. Finally, you find it impossible to recover what you have with your partner. Next thing you know, you're splitting up.

The idea is to do the opposite. Value your sexual relationship above all else. Make time for making love. Don't let too much time pass between you without making a sexual connection. Keep kissing. Kissing is an exchange of hormones that heightens your sexual drive and focus.

Keep sex a current topic. Talk about sex for 5 minutes every day. Read up on sex. It is well documented that a passionate, intimate, healthy sex life is the key to long-term relationships.

No loving couple can afford to neglect the sex. This is the basic secret to an intimate sexual relationship. No matter how much money you make and the effort, energy and time it takes to make it, there is an essential rule in life here. You can't buy what a great sex life gives you. It is so valuable, that to neglect your sex life, or think it isn't as important as your work-out in the gym or playing eighteen holes on the golf course is erroneous. Which is the complete opposite of erogenous! Neglecting the bedroom is one of the biggest mistakes you can make.

Why is a sex life so important? Sex is vital to keeping your relationship together. Without sharing great sex, a couple can become disconnected to the point where they're just not into each other anymore. Then little by little you stop sharing most things in your relationship. You become so distant you can't see what you are as a couple anymore.

MAKE LOVE NOT WAR

DON'T SLEEP WITH THE ENEMY.

You know the saying: "Make Love Not War". Fights in themselves are not destructive things. How you both deal with a conflict of ideas or values, is where you get into problems. Let's face it, you are two individuals. You don't want to feel that you must always agree to keep the peace. And why should you. You're going to see things differently and not agree on everything. But why does a minor discussion turn into major conflict so easily?

Blanshard & Blanshard have worked out that fights are emotional fireworks. Partners throw a few verbal crackers past each other. Let off a barrage of spinning incendiary thoughts, use searing sky-rockets to highlight unresolved issues. In the basic science of arguments words and actions create uncensored explosions.

Issues in relationships are bound to come up. Unchecked, small issues can be used as ammunition to get at your partner for all the myriad of ways they annoy you. And all the previous little things you let them get away with. But if you mask the issue with a verbal slam and start attacking your partners worth; the fight becomes an excuse for dealing with your partner in a way that causes resentment and annoyance.

OK. So you share your most personal thoughts and your body with your partner. And what happens? Inside this intimate setting, your partner does a 180° change in attitude towards you, a snappy answer will do it. Right at the start of any disagreement you know if it's going to be more than a discussion. You recognise subtle signs in body language and the manner and tone of what's being said. The fight is in it's infancy and you know it. At that point of knowing, you have to make a decision about which direction you want to go. Into the positive problem solving discussion mode, or into the negative 'let's have this out now' battle stance.

Now it feels like you're sleeping with the enemy. It can happen at the end of a day when personal reserves are low; the air becomes heavy, feelings become confused, dare we say it even nasty. Things are said, you retaliate. Now there's hostility. This is the partner you can't stand. Or understand. The uniqueness of your love, is now questionable. Who likes feeling less than perfect. Who doesn't take alarm at the first signs of blame. When it's pointed out that we are nothing less than infallible; we turn around and contradict, argue, justify, incriminate, rage, cry...do anything but give in to a partner who's pointed out your mistake.

Other arguments are started by a partner who is frustrated with not being heard or feels they are not getting enough two-way talk. You want to remain close, yet sometimes someone does not understand your needs and feelings. So they tend to minimise, or trivialize what you say. Someone thinks everything is fine. Yet you feel bad. When your partner avoids talking things over, you feel emotionally or verbally unheard and frustrated. You start complaining. You complain to flash a focus on what's bothering you, so they can see there is a problem. After all, you both have to admit a problem exists to solve it.

Notice how often, you argue about small issues but there is also a dangerous undercurrent of unresolved issues that keep surging into the latest disagreement. Then your simple disagreement turns into an argument that rages out of control.

Unresolved differences and grievances progress rapidly into a desire to slam the door on your intimate and physical relationship. The idea is not to accumulate a dossier of issues.

So how do we fix things when bad feelings have shut the relationship down to a point where you'd rather eat dirt than say something nice to each other! It's actually quiet simple. It only takes one person to start discussions and close the gap between you. If you are not good at making the first move to talk, after a volatile argument, then respect the courage it takes for your partner to open the lines of communication. When you start the discussion avoid being critical. Give up the blame game. Maintain respect for each other.

Take the time to talk about whatever is on your mind. Conflicts get resolved by talking honestly. Once you do, you'll start sharing all your inner thoughts with renewed truthfulness. This disclosure of feelings moves the relationship into deeper love.

So don't be afraid to lay it all out. Make the most of an argument. Talk it through when you are calmer but still intense. You'll have energy and passion to do it. Use this energy to work it out. A productive fight ends in a resolution in which each person understands the other's point of view.

How you handle the fighting is where you make or eventually break your relationship. What makes a relationship work is this. If you clarify feelings and work them out together, you will notice renewed romantic vibes and sexual connection. Intimacy creates more intimacy. When you talk and feel truly understood and accepted, the gates to the heavenly side of your love open again. You trust each other again. The great feelings of love return.

FINGERPRINTS

POINTING THE FINGER OF BLAME.

YOU piss me off, YOU forgot to, YOU remind me of, YOU said, YOU lost my, YOU didn't remember, YOU promised, YOU left the, YOU can't do that. Pointing the finger of blame is a sure way to kill any conversation about issues you wish to talk about. The most finger pointing word in the dictionary is YOU.

Once you are aware of how much finger pointing, blame, and accusations belongs to the word YOU; you can do something about saying what you mean without sounding accusational.

Don't go pinning all the blame on your partner. Or bringing up random shortcomings that are irrelevant. Don't chip away at your partner for minor 'crimes'. Instinctively, the slightest touch of blame, moves you like a chess piece into a protective position of self-justification. You arm yourself with words, retort and prepare to fight back. If the discussion turns to finger pointing, you're heading for a fight.

What is easy, is to find fault with your partner! No one is perfect and no one should point the finger. You know you may be the one at fault. If you take the attitude that you're only 50% responsible, think again. If you know you're wrong, accept it. Don't try and shift the responsibility to someone else. Accept 100% responsibility for the situation and save both of you a great deal of angst.

Blame no one and your problem solving capabilities as a couple improve dramatically. When this happens, you'll make positive changes and discover new ways to relate to each other.

BLOW

AVOIDING THE RELATIONSHIP BLOWOUT.

You can reverse the slide towards relationship blowout, where stress and bad feelings are a prelude to a broken heart ending.

Keep in mind, whatever issues you have right now can be resolved. Without problems, there can't be growth in your relationship. What matters about problems is what you do with them.

So the first step in creating a long term relationship is to get honest with yourself and each other. It's not going to be easy. You know why? As human beings, we have a great capacity to lie, tell half and quarter truths and be manipulative. Deception is the enemy.

A relationship is not a place to aerate your lies. If you lie to avoid confrontation, keep the peace or to get our own way. Soon your partner won't be able to rely on you. Rather than hiding the grit of reality and putting up a fake false front, be honest. Tell it as it is. Your truth. That way you'll be a straight thinker.

Live authentically and be true to yourself. Say what you're really thinking. If you hide things to protect yourself or to make your partner feel better, then your partner will get the feeling you're not being truthful, and sure enough you're not. Suspicion creates an invisible line between you. And suspicion makes your relationship questionable, because your lover doesn't honestly know where they stand.

Secondly, look at issues that keep re-surfacing, repeating and staying unresolved. These unresolved issues are like thorns in the heart of your relationship. Unless you work them out, they have a way of working in deeper. When issues involving anger or a real need to control happen- sexual fulfillment gets interrupted until these issues are resolved. That is why it's essential to take time to focus on issues.

Fights are not a sign of weakness or breakdown, in your relationship. Instead of worrying about how many times you argue, worry about how you argue. Remember two things. Love is a renewable resource. Relationships are all about love.

DOUBLE TROUBLE

LIGHTNING CAN STRIKE TWICE.

Double trouble. This is where life throws problems in your direction: like your car breaking down, the dog running away. Then a serious life issue you didn't see coming: severe illness, losing your job or losing your home. Some things throw your life into chaos.

These extremely trying times test your reserves as a couple to the maximum. You can feel like two separate people, coping in your own way with life's dramas. As they unfold, you forget to look after the relationship. Until eventually you no longer fall back on each other for support when you need it most. Or worse, blame each other for the situation or outcome.

In times of crisis, you can start to lose the very person who needs you and whom you need. You lose yourselves in the stress and turmoil. We all experience hard and difficult times throughout our lives, none of us are immune, but you can come out with your relationship still intact.

Accept that you have strong emotions. But don't be tempted to throw any negativity in your partners direction. If you do, you risk having a couple's argument on top of your current personal situation. Instead, make an effort to let feelings come and go. Don't act on them. Don't involve your partner until you have clarity. And when you do you'll have a friend there to discuss it with! When you suffer major life crisis, it's doubly important to look after each other. Then your relationship won't be a casualty of your circumstances.

DOG & BONE

BURYING THE ARGUMENT AND DIGGING IT UP LATER.

Are you like a dog with the proverbial bone? Do you have difficulty letting go? Do you bury things that have been said, only to dig it up later and have another go! Do you pretend to accept apologies? Tell them you forgive them, but know you won't forget. Or do you forgive and remember. For every new arguments, and let the unburied ghosts on other battlefields join the fight. In another argument, you find yourself digging up dirt from a past scene and splicing them all together.

You produce the same words your partner said a few days before, or months or years, in order to contradict what they are saying. By displacing, disjointing words, and sentences, by misunderstanding the whole, or quoting only part of what was said, you may show up their inconsistencies. But you won't show them your capacity for love. Based on how your partner reacts, you may harass and provoke regular fights, thinking you gain a little at a time to get the upper hand.

Slamming doors, breaking things, shouting. Name calling. Packing your bags, driving off at top speed. Or calling a cab for the airport within earshot. Hold on a minute! That's when a disagreement escalates into a scene. One scene follows another, until your relationship is like a sad B grade movie. A bad, ugly, embarrassing one you've produced! Fights that let rip, escalate into dramas which build up and accumulate in your mind. Each scene is about you as a couple. The more you argue, the more negative dossiers, scripts and files collect in your memory. These compound dramas fracture loving relationships. Dramas are the sticks and stones that damage what you have. Dramas have the power to write themselves into memory. The memory of bad times weighs heavily on the relationship, burying beautiful loving feelings. If you could take photographs of dramas you have created, they would be black and heavy. You'd have a big black year book of bad feelings.

Accumulating bad feelings is not the aim of a long term loving relationship. Arguments that attack on a personal level are destructive enough to destroy love. In that case, there are no winners. You both lose big time. Every emotional scene you make is distressing and every scene you participate in has the potential to end the relationship. You never know which drama will be the deciding factor for your partner. The point when they have had enough of you! An emotional tipping point where you can't go back to how things were. Every uncensored argument breaks down good feelings between you. Too many dramas and couples are ready to sign each other out of their lives. Go figure!

Intelligent loving means you road block any arguments before they turn into a drama. If you can't let things go, make sure you prevent them escalating into major dramas. You have it in your power to stop high drama. Apply the 30 minute rule. After 30 minutes, when disagreements are going nowhere, STOP.

Take some physical time-out from each other. Agree to talk about it in 1 hours time. Get back together. Talk for 30 minutes. STOP. If you still haven't figured it out leave it. Arrange an exact time and perhaps another day to talk about the issue. After 30 minutes, apply the 30 minute rule again.

When something is agreed, after a fight /discussion, post resolution of said fight, the subject should never be raised again in the same context. Know when to let go. Letting go doesn't mean you dig the parts up months later. You just let it go.

BEDROOM RULES

SOME RULES ARE NOT
TO BE BROKEN.

There's going to be conflict in any relationship. The trick is the timing. Sort out issues during the day and don't drag them into your bedroom. Never use the bed or bedroom for discussing anything negative. Turning out the light and arguing in the dark is a major mistake couples make. You can spend three hours arguing about what could be decided in three minutes.

An important thing to remember: you've heard the saying, don't go to bed without making up. Well it's true. If you go to sleep angry, unresolved conflict goes into your psyche where it accumulates on a deeper level and stalks your relationship from the shadows. You can't mentally identify it, but you find yourself reacting in volatile ways towards your partner. This can happen months later and you really can't understand where these bad feelings are coming from. That's why it's vital to resolve conflict on the day you argue. So don't go to bed angry. Keep your bedroom vibes sexy.

FOUR SIDES

HOW TO GET OUT
OF THE ARGUMENT BOX.

A Couple's argument has four sides. In any disagreement, you can identify The Perpetrator, The Avenger, The Rescuer and The Victim.

Arguments don't start by themselves. First, you have The Perpetrator who is upset or outraged about something. They might have held their feelings inside but reach a flash point where they must say something. Before you know it's a house fire. The timing doesn't matter. What The Perpetrator says to The Victim (who may have their feet up reading a book and relaxing) turns The Victim into The Avenger.

The Avenger's automatic reaction is to get pay-back. When this happens, The Perpetrator, (remember, the one who brought up the issue in the first place) seeing the anger they have caused, starts to feel guilty. On sensing this, The Perpetrator quickly becomes The Rescuer.

The Rescuer feels bad about what is happening, and at the same time, frustrated at trying to fix the problem. The solution for The Rescuer, is to take the role of The Victim. How insane is that!

Now Pandora's Box of arguments is laid out flat, you can both step outside the square!

WIRED FOR SEX

ARE YOU HOT WIRED FOR SEX?

The human brain is wired for sex. All nerve endings in your body travel the neuron super-pathway and end up in your brain. Having sex, floods your brain with chemicals that make you feel great.

Sex has been proven to be great for overall health of body, mind, and spirit. Having great sex energizes you both physically and emotionally. You get so many great benefits: antidepressant, beautifying, longevity, anti-stress, analgesic as a bonus. And all for free! Sex restores your energy levels. Right after you make love, notice how your energy levels rise.

Your body is physically geared up for sex. Use it or lose it! Sex keeps your hormones in balance. After sex, a woman produces more estrogen. So sex, even just once a week, regulates the menstrual cycle, increases fertility and delays menopause symptoms. Recent studies point to the fact that regular sex helps reduce the risk of prostate cancer.

Sex is a natural drugstore, the best panacea against depression. Why? Researchers have documented a release of feel good chemicals which dulls pain and reduces stress levels. Sex is a natural high. It elevates your mood up when you're feeling down. A recent study found that lovers who engage in regular sex, had significantly lower rates of depression than people who didn't have regular sex.

Sex is better than aspirin. It's the headache-free card! When you have the proverbial, "not tonight I've got a headache," instead of turning away, have sex!

If you can over-ride your headache enough to make love, your hormones levels will increase. Hormones produced, by having sex, are potent enough to take pain away. So, in effect, your partner has the power to take your headache away. And vice versa. You'll both wake up refreshed and deal to the problems that gave you that thumping headache in the first place.

Life-saver Sex: Statistics show that you will live longer and stay in better shape if you are having sex.

Life-guard Sex: Revives, rejuvenates. Sex can reduce the risk of stroke. Sex helps the body fight free-radicals and so assists the anti-aging process.

Specialist Sex: Proven to reduce the risk of breast and prostate cancer.

Doctor Sex: Helps the body heal cuts, fight infection, mend deep wounds and repair bruised tissues, supports red and white blood cells, oxygenates blood, helps promote bone growth, repairs cells and renews tissues, and promotes circulation for healthy skin. Sex boosts you immune system.

Psychologist Sex: Improves memory and cognitive skills. Your lover will greatly appreciate the bliss in your relationship. Great sex works both ways, You feel great and your partner does too.

Personal Trainer Sex: Makes you more flexible, boosts your metabolism helping you burn fat quicker. And stay hard core.

Blanshard & Blanshard: Call it free love! The more sex you have, the more you get back for free. Love Sex. Love Life.

THE ART OF SEX

SEX IS THE ULTIMATE CREATIVE FORCE.

Every time you make love you are engaging in what is arguably one of the most creative pursuits known. Great poems, writings, artwork, music have been born from the power of sex and its profound effect on the human spirit and psyche.

Creative people are into sex, big time: musicians, artists, scientists, visionaries, leaders, movie stars! For them, making love is essential. Great sex creates great ideas, art and music. Sex is the ultimate creative force. After all sex creates life itself. The procreation of life, ideas and ideals begin with sex.

You can be creative during sex too, the way you think up new positions, techniques, and places to make love in. The more time you spend being creative, the more sexually powered up you feel. The more sexy you are, the more creative vibes you have.

If you want to create a flow of creative ideas in your life, solve problems or generate new ideas, have sex. Ideas get born and life becomes more creative.

THE EROTIC KITCHEN

LOVE IS A BANQUET.
DON'T GO HUNGRY.

Sex benefits your relationship, both in and out of the bedroom. Having a store of erotic feelings gained from making love, helps you cope with the not-so-great parts of your life. Starve each other of a physical relationship and you'll feel empty of love. When this happens you need to up your sex quota. Make love more and you will feel more in love. Get back in touch.

Through the day we lay our hands on so much man made stuff. Sometimes we just need to get real and lay our hands on the stuff of man and woman. Or man man or woman woman or multiples of the above.

Spend more intimate hours in the soft warmth of each others arms. Put dirty sex in your day. Notice how small stuff, ego issues, seem to matter less. Love is a banquet. Indulge. Don't go hungry or run on empty.

BRAIN FOREPLAY

EXPERIENCE SIX TIMES THE ORGASM.

You can experience six times the orgasm, when you practise the art of seducing each other. Latest research shows that slow, tantalising, drawn-out foreplay releases key hormones in the brain, testosterone in a man, estrogen in a woman, dopamine and oxytocin in both. When testosterone, estrogen, dopamine and oxytocin come together the result is orgasm central: explosive orgasms, simultaneous and multiple orgasms.

Experiencing a sexually charged orgasm in the evening, happens as simply as brewing an espresso coffee in the morning. As soon as you wake up, get your dirty thoughts going. Starting you day with sexy thoughts, puts your mind in foreplay.

Foreplay serves an important purpose in the art of seduction. You trigger sex hormones that make great orgasm possible later. You can leave things for the imagination -

whether it's whispering innuendos, or leaving a sexy note on a pillow. Maintain a sexual connection with your partner. Try a sexy, direct statement, that says "I want you". Then watch the tempo go up after the usual hug and kiss. It doesn't take much to get someone thinking about sexy possibilities. You know what gets them excited and keeps them turned on.

Maintaining a sexual connection during the day keeps a strong sense of sexuality outside of the bedroom. Sending a sexy text message or surprising them with a sexually loaded compliment. It's all about not holding back. Lovers are not mind readers. Flirting with your partner is part of seduction. Seduce and let loose! Anything you do or say that creates erotic anticipation, has the effect of foreplay on the brain. You can be apart during the day and already boosting dopamine levels that amp up your partners libido...the urges that make you want to make love. Dopamine increases, the hormone responsible for creating physical and sexual excitement. Happy orgasm! And many happy returns!

DOING SEX

SEX IS A MIRROR REFLECTION OF HOW YOU'RE DOING LIFE.

Sex is the greatest asset to your relationship. How you do sex is a metaphor for how you do life. Sex is like a mirror reflecting habits, patterns and survival strategies seen in other areas of your life.

You know when its time to change the habits of a sexual lifetime. When life becomes so boring you start to lose interest in doing it. You just need to pay more attention to what you are doing in the sex department.

Great sex is not about specific technique. Standing on your head. Swinging from the chandelier. Missionary position, lotus, warrior, down-dog up-dog. A skilled lover isn't someone who knows every position in the book, it's the lover who is fully in the moment, generous with their feelings and not holding back.

When you give full attention to your partner, you write your own chapters together. Intimacy, love, trust, passion, hot sex and whatever turns you on. Sexual and sensual liaisons give you more than physical pleasure. You find yourself sharing a deep limitless connection with your partner. This happens when both physical and emotional elements are in the right position.

You can have sex on the shag-pile, in an office chair, on the kitchen table. Sitting. Standing. By trying different positions, you can see which ones you both like. You might even discover that one position brings you to orgasm over and over again.

Keep sex charged up and exciting. By changing the moves you change the mood. You develop your own sexual style in bed together, but you can grow and expand your repertoire. Learn new positions and techniques. Experiment. Try something different, by mutual consent. Everyone has their own pleasure, so don't be restricted by a particular technique. The position that works best for one partner, is often not the other's favorite position, and vice versa. So it's important not to get stuck in someone's favorite velvet rut! This can happen if one partner is more definite about what they want. Variety is the spice of love life. So even if you have a great sexy routine going together, find new and exciting ways to do it.

THE CUDDLE HORMONE

HOW TO SUPER SIZE YOUR ORGASM.

Every time you touch each other, you release a powerhouse of the hormone oxytocin - the cuddle hormone. Oxytocin makes you feel more connected to each other. Hormones have the ability to super-size your orgasms too. Oxytocin floods the brain during climax and scientists think it may be responsible for giving you the tingly all over sensation. The more you touch each other with skin to skin contact, the more the hormone accumulates. Combine it with the glut of testosterone for him, estrogen for her, dopamine and you have the fuel to intensify your orgasms. The final spike of dopamine comes when you touch each other.

No matter how long you've been together, you never

outgrow your need to be in touch. Your skin is the biggest sensory organ you have, yet it's often forgotten about. Textures such as silk, fur, feather and satin can help you stay in touch with touch. Being touched in sensual, sexual, and caring ways makes you feel relaxed, loving, and loveable. Couples who do have sex often, show more feelings. They touch, kiss, hug more and have fewer problems between them. They often show their feelings in public. Why? Sex makes the body produce more oxytocin - the hormone that makes us feel the need to care and trust someone.

DIRTY CHAT

TALK ABOUT THE GOOD
THE BAD AND THE
FANTASTIC.

If you two have been together awhile, it might be time for a dirty chat! What gives you pleasure, needs to be talked about. What feels exquisite to you in lovemaking, how you like to play, secrets of foreplay and more. Your partner is not a mind reader. Sex is a relevant topic in a relationship.

We can spend more time talking about work and money than sharing intimate talk. Money comes and goes. Your relationship is like your personal bank of intimate feelings. You both make withdrawals and deposits. So it's worth checking, what's hot or not. Who's in the red. Who's in the black and while we're on the subject, a small gift when it isn't a birthday. Untie a satin ribbon, perfume or flowers, sharing a bath for two, a bottle of wine. Just because your sex life is fine, it doesn't mean that you should take it for granted.

Partners feel connected and more in tune with each other, when they are free to give and say and show what they want and like. Show and tell! Yes! Moaning in the moment and making sounds is a good thing! Using your breath turns on your own natural responses and self expression. Sexual self confidence happens when you communicate in bed. Tell your partner exactly how it feels. In this way you learn how unlimited sex is. You'll discover how you can make love with the same lover a thousand times and yet the lovemaking always feels different and new!

SEX IN YOUR CITY

MAKE A DATE WITH YOUR PARTNER.

What if you can't afford the time to take a vacation? Or your holidays aren't due for months. Make a plan that only includes the two of you. Have sex in your own city. Check into a hotel.

Think about the fact that tourists spend thousands of dollars to get to the city you are living in. Take advantage of having sex in your city. One night in Bangkok. Sleepless in Seattle or Paris. When you are living in a place, you are already there. You don't have to travel to be the tourist.

The rest is up to your imagination. Check into a local hotel for the sheer pleasure of getting away from your house or apartment. Share the bath, the thousand thread count on freshly ironed sheets, feather pillows and room service. Or red light blinking neon outside the motel window. Take a day off. Take off for the day, or a weekend, just be together. Long, luxurious, sexy, creative, affordable dates. Whatever works for you as a couple reviver. You and your partner will learn to love your dedicated time together and make every moment count. When you make time to make love, you feel more connected, more bonded, more intimate, more passion and more together. The intimacy between you is unlimited.

ONE SENTENCE

STOP GOING OVER AND OVER THE BAD TIMES IN YOUR LIFE STORY.

As a couple you experience good times and bad. When you talk about the good times together, those thoughts trigger feel-good chemicals. But, if you talk about the stressful times, like the time when you lost your job, or when your business went under, or the family crisis. By the time you finish talking over the past, it creates a cocktail of stress chemicals in your body. You will feel as stressed out as when the event took place. You feel miserable again. If you find that a few words trigger you to go back over the worst times of your lives then give up talking about the bad times. It can be an addiction. But giving up is actually easier than you think.

First become aware of the topics you drag up and

chew over a lot. Next be aware of the words for the topic, like: lawyer, boss, business, friend, lover, illness, children, mother, mortgage, bank. Then, when you are talking about the past and recognise a key trigger word, say out loud to your partner these words: "One Sentence." Which means they can say one sentence about the stressful topic. And one sentence only. They must stop talking about the trigger topic. And neither of you pursue the topic at that point in time. This stops the ruminating in endless discussions over past events that you can't change, no matter how many times you bring them up and go over them. Some things just make you feel sad and bad.

If either of you want to talk about major past issues, don't sneak them into your conversation. If you want to discuss a key trigger topic, ask permission from your partner to talk about an issue. So they can be mentally prepared and emotionally ready to discuss it.

Whatever you do, don't talk about the sad, bad times in your bed. Find a place outside the house to talk over negative stressful issues. Keep your house for positive times. Then you won't end up filling your living environment up with negativity. Bad feelings and memories in a house or apartment is the number one reason why most people move house!

CINNAMON SEX

THERE'S MORE SIN
IN CINNAMON

What has cinnamon got to do with great sex? Intensely aromatic spices like cinnamon, nutmeg, aniseed, cloves and ginger stay in your body and perfume your mouth and other parts! So you can actually alter the way you taste. And make your French kisses hot!

So there is more to a mouthful of cinnamon bun than you imagine. *Blanshard & Blanshard* knew a couple who spent long afternoons in bed. The secret was cinnamon, cardamom, star anise, cloves and nutmeg with their spicy scents. This couple found these culinary discoveries and sexual delicacies while living in Southern India. They literally spiced up their love-life.

Smell and taste are important senses in the bedroom. It is no secret that the use of spices in teas, wine and food has been known for centuries. Traders on the ancient spice route bought and sold precious powders, pods and bark for silver and gold. And it is said that sailors could guide there ships towards land, by the perfume of spices growing on the shores of the islands. Today, spices are found in the isles of supermarkets.

Some spices are still rare and exotic. It takes 75,000 flowers to make one pound of saffron, the dried stigmas of a flower, making it the most expensive spice in the world at over $200 an ounce. The delicate stigmas have a powerful bitter and sweet honey taste. Licorice, fennel, star anise. Peppery, spicy, piquant. Cinnamon apple tart. Strong warm hot ginger tea. From the kitchen to the bedroom. Discover exotic spices and have sexual adventures on the spice route.

SMART SEX

TWO BRAINS ARE BETTER THAN ONE.

The love part of the brain and the sex part are different. When you understand the differences you'll realize why you love sex.

The human brain has a huge limbic system. And the limbic part of our brain wants one thing. All it wants is sex! For you to get down and do it! That's all the limbic system cares about. So figure that you have a huge part of your brain wanting nothing but s-e-x. While another part of the human brain, the cortex, is all about love.

The cortex socializes sex. It produces feelings like deep love and caring for someone. The cortex is at the heart center of love and loving feelings. It's the reason we write love. The cortex of our brain moves us to express our feelings: hugging, kissing, gentle touches, whispering softly. Foreplay is made of this. Then from all the cortex loving you feel, your limbic turns on and you totally submit to each other, having great limbic fired sex and the pleasure of total passion as that instinctual level of hormones shimmer in your body and zillions of neurons fire off in your brain.

The more you know someone the harder it is to get onto the limbic level. Your cortex with its loving social responsibilities can get in the way. That's why, some people find it impossible to have true limbic sex with their partners after three or four years of being together. While on the other hand many people prefer to have cortical sex for five or six years. Then when they finally get comfortable and secure, they go limbic. So sometimes the timing between partners gets screwed up.

If you understand what is happening, you can adjust your limbic and cortex brains to get in sync with each other. More foreplay for the cortex and more dirty action for the limbic.

SEX UNPLUGGED

TURN OFF YOUR SMART PHONE AND TURN ON YOUR SEX LIFE.

You're out together, you're planning on having a great time :) you're there with your partner :) you're probably at a café, pressing your lips against your second cup of coffee, imported from Italy, dark roast, you've probably kicked your shoes off and your partner is scrolling/down/ messages/on mobile :(

Get real. You're sitting, waiting, waiting, and you're gonna wait for an hour or three lattes later. Your partner is too busy texting to notice you; convince yourself that they are entitled to spend time texting, talking on their latest mobile, new icons, new program does this and push this, does that, index finger scrolls down, I won't be a minute, while you are pretending to be happy, (who are you to be jealous of small things like electronic devices), who is this person they're talking to now, call waiting, take a message, send one anyway, sorry I've got to take this call, oh hi how are things. Who are you to complain, you've got better things to think about anyway, there is always work to be done. Open lap top. That feels better, well, you have a million things to do, make appointments for tomorrow, so many things need attention, important things right? So listen, it's getting late, are you ready to go? So modern. So cyber. So not sexy.

Seriously, turn off the phone. Turn off the electronics. It's a robotic anti-sex plot. Close the laptop. Now you're ready to get down and get human. Geeks don't have as much real sex. Cyber fact.

THE ISLAND

ARE YOU OCEANS APART?

You've heard the saying: No woman is an island unto herself. No man is either. It's a big, lonely world out there when you're on your own. You can be in a relationship and yet feel like you are oceans apart.

Partner: That's a great looking island!
Partner: No response
Partner: Well, It'd be a great place to go for a vacation, don't you think?
Partner: Silence
Partner: Well, what do you think of my butt?
Partner: No response

If you're not listening, you make your partner feel like a bore and they end up running monologue after monologue because you don't react. If you ignore or reply from behind a book, or don't look up from your laptop, if you walk into another room or talk on your mobile phone, while your partner is talking. If you ignore your partner like this, you'll end up on the proverbial desert island, alone. Through silence or non-participation, you are saying a hell of a lot. What you don't realize is how damaging this vacuum is to the relationship. Your partner interprets your vacant sign as this: what you are doing is more important than what your partner is saying.

What causes this separation? Fear. Although you may not admit it. Sometimes we separate ourselves by making a mental note to avoid certain subjects, because from past experience, they lead to arguments. So you remain silent.

Criticism is another reason we find it difficult to talk. No one likes to be criticised. When your partner constantly offers you unasked for advice, they are being obtusely critical of you. You suspect as much and so you say nothing again. That silent strategy is starting to set you adrift on your island of silence. You appear vague, remote and disinterested. And faraway.

Silence is a distancing style of behaviour. You both need to work this out. Communication goes both ways. Specific things you say or do encourage natural responses within your partner that make then want to be intimate with you. Saying the wrong thing, or not saying anything, can leave your partner feeling emotionally detached from you.

When your partner shares their feelings, listen to what's on their mind. Not being listened to, is like someone not seeing you for who you are or even worse... of no importance and so not even worthy of a reply. The inability to listen and talk with your partner carries a poignant loss. You really don't know the person you are in love with. If you stop talking, you lose each other. It doesn't have to go this way.

Express yourself and be open to the self-expressions of others. When opinions are listened to and seen as valid, you'll both feel you can talk about anything. We are talking animals and this talk keeps us together. Listen to each other and talk from the heart.

THE ZOO

ARE YOU STILL
A TIGER/TIGRESS IN BED

Do you remember when you first met you called each other names like tiger, chickie-babe and cuddles. Nick-names make our relationship feel private. More secret. That's the way it is. Lovers rename each other. But what about those names you call each other now?

There's a saying: In the first year of a relationship, one partner listens to the other. In the second year of a relationship, the other partner listens. In the third year, the neighbours listen to them both and they're hearing a four letter word and it isn't Love. Now it's mixed up with those other less endearing four letter words built into phrases like, Cow. Ass. Ape. Snake. Don't call each other names. Even if for a moment your partner embodies every character of an animal. It is scraping the bottom of the cage to refer to someone you love, as zoo-doo.

Remember, you can't undo or unsay what you've

said. Often what is said is untrue and exaggerated purely to inflict pain. When you blurt something out at your partner, you inflict emotional pain. When you pursue a take-no-prisoners approach to your arguments, your partner hears you loud and clear. Or when you abandon the issue and attack the worth of your partner. You risk damaging or permanently destroying your relationship. When you say something destructive and later say, "I didn't really mean it." "Of course it's not true." "I was just being mean." Too late! What's said can't be unsaid. So make a pledge to never fire off your mouth in an argument again. It's about self control.

MOUNT G SPOT

HIGH ALTITUDE SEX INTENSIFIES YOUR ORGASM.

When planning your next vacation together don't forget the G-spot. There are geographic spots on the map that can improve your sex life. High-altitude sex in the mountains or alps can significantly increase pleasure sensations and this can make for more intense orgasms. The higher you and your partner get above sea level, the less oxygen is in the air. At 8,000 feet, the oxygen level decreases considerably. You find yourself breathing faster, your heart rate is higher and your body adjusts its blood chemistry.

Mind-blowing sex at a high altitude is not a problem that needs a cure, so research into its causes and workings has not been extensive. So trust *Blanshard & Blanshard* to do their own research. *Blanshard & Blanshard* traveled to Leadville, Colorado, the highest altitude town in the United States. Evenings at 12,000 feet above sea level, they both reported more intense orgasms. It's possible that they may have been experiencing a bit of oxygen-constricted intensity. It's also possible that in addition to some altitude-induced sensitivity they may have been exhilarated by the experience of having sex in a new place, the mundane concerns of daily life left far below the mountain peaks. Whatever the case, they found a new G-spot.

Next stop, K2!

THE BAD PATCH

ROUGH TIMES CAN STRENGTHEN YOUR LOVE.

People often ask us, is falling in love and staying in love with the same person really possible? Or do you just show them the door?

How do you move past those bad days where love is going to pieces and you have no idea why. You're arguing all the time. Even on Valentine's Day! Arguably the most romantic day of the year. You're just not getting on anymore. While this sounds bad it doesn't mean the relationship is over. It's just a bad patch.

Perhaps you have begun to avoid sex entirely due to a backlog of incomplete communication. Perhaps you feel the need for variety but don't want to go outside the relationship for it. Sex is a powerful element in a relationships and having a great sexual relationship means you can work through any issues. Because sex repairs, heals and balances emotional equilibrium. So don't neglect or overlook intimate sexual experiences and how important they are. You can deal with any issue, loss, tragedy, anything life throws at you. At the end of the day, sexual intimacy is the currency you need to get through bad patches and hard times.

But be aware, when you are going through any crisis, you must keep looking after your relationship. If you are going through a bad patch imagine that you and your partner are in the middle of a circle. It is just you and your partner there. No family, no friends, no one but yourselves together. No matter what situation you have to cope with, don't let outside problems, pain or hurt come into the circle you have made.

Everyone faces bad times in relationships. While you're having bad times, it's important to keep in mind, that this situation, this moment in time, is not permanent. No matter how impossible it seems. Try and stay cool and spend this uncomfortable time working it out instead of freaking out. Given time and a desire to stay together, every issue can be solved or resolved.

Make an effort to shift any negative energy that is enveloping you from outside your relationship. You can do this in a practical way by stopping and deciding to do one good thing together. Even if you don't feel like it. It's really important to redirect yourselves in a positive way. You've got to add good things. Good things balance out negativity. This is where the red roses and chocolates do work. So do moonlight and candlelight. They help diffuse tense situations. By their nature they soften shadows and harsh lines. Romantic elements add a sensual dimension to difficult times.

When things feel heavy, make a move, do something sensual together. That's essential. When you're back to sharing good times again, you'll realize that the bad patch was a necessary adjustment. You didn't walk out the door, you stayed together.

The bad patch was a good thing because it strengthened and moved the relationship on. There is a massive difference between a short-term relationship and a long-term relationship. In short-term relationships partners walk out during bad patches. In long-term relationships, they don't.

SEXY NEURONS

FIRE OFF NEURONS AND
FIRE UP YOUR LOVE LIFE.

Everything we do fires off neurons in the brain and that makes us feel good. Take a bath and you fire off maybe 12 neurons, watching a great movie maybe you'll fire 69, reading a French magazine 90, reading Watermark by Joseph Brodsky 185, watching a butterfly 287, eating a smoked salmon bagel maybe 320, eating a bowl of fettuccine 800, if watching a world famous Cirque 1530, if lying in a hammock 2000, if strumming a guitar 2205, if snowboarding in fresh powder 3500, if swimming in topical blue water around 4600, but when you have an orgasm, millions and millions and millions and millions and millions of neuron cells fire off in your brain! Nothing can beat that!

Neurons in the brain signal the release of endorphins. How happy you feel, is dependent on the amount of endorphins released into the bloodstream. When you fall in love, you have an above average level of endorphins and that's why you feel so incredibly happy. It is also why some people who get addicted to the feelings of endorphin highs leave their partner to get a rush, with a new lover.

The truth is you don't have to go to that much trouble. All you need on a daily basis to make yourself feel happy, is to power up more endorphins! It's possible to do. You use an extremely powerful narcotic called thinking positively. There is a negative and positive way to look at most things. If you use positive thinking as a narcotic, then the line of positive thought can produce a surge of endorphins. If you feel negative, this doesn't create a sense of well-being for yourself or the people around you. Tell yourself that you're very happy for a moment, which might be a lie and it might not. The thing is, your brain won't know the difference. By creating the illusion in your brain, the brain will believe it and you top up your endorphin levels. So when you are feeling bad about anything, don't make yourself worse by continuing negative thoughts on the subject. Stop for a moment and tell yourself the opposite. Tell yourself that you're in love with your work, in love with your friends, in love with that person you had an argument with.

When an issue comes up, check your level of happiness and up your endorphin levels. Take the positive side. Then add another boost of natural endorphins in the form of an exercise, sex, a warm bath, shower, swim, a long walk, massage, yoga, weight-lifting, laughing, drawing, painting, writing. Everything you do makes a difference to how you think. Everything you think makes a difference to how you feel.

LOVE SCENTS

MAKING SENSE OF SCENTS.

Sometimes relationship problems are there under your noses. Sometimes you simply need to get away from each other!

There is a tiny gland called the sebaceous gland that releases chemicals on the skin's surface which produces a scent on the skin. When you first get together the attraction to this subtle scent is high. Your partner literally gets all over you. They're in your hair, in the air, they're in the sheets; they're even in the towels. They're in your wardrobe on everything you wear.

The more your apartment fills with each others chemicals, the more neutralised these become. There is no longer a feeling of other. As this happens, sharing, loving, working together becomes asexual. So you need to recognise when this is happening.

If you're kissing and it's not happening for you, it's

time to detoxify! Yes! You read that right! Take a physical break from each other. The detoxification period is at least three to four weeks and both partners have to get away. If one partner stays at home and the other travels, the partner at home is still surrounded by all the same chemicals.

So what can you do if you can't get away? Clean the house! Change the sheets on the bed. Change the fabric softener you use on your clothes, change your perfume, change your aftershave. Change the scent of body-wash or soaps for the shower and bath. Add scented aromatherapy oils in a diffuser with sensual oils that enhance erotic desire: ylang ylang, sandalwood, or patchouli. Use an ionizer, air purifier and freshen your environment. Don't forget vases of fresh cut flowers. Think musk of roses or tie up a bundle of lemongrass and surround with limes in a dish.

Change all the scents in the house. Then your senses will be alive to each other, as though you had just met.

INTIMACY

RED LACE PANTIES ARE CLASSIFIED INTIMATE APPAREL.

What is intimacy exactly? There are many forms of intimacy. A whisper in someone's ear is intimate. Red lace panties are classified intimate apparel. Then there is intimate behaviour. Kissing, touching, lovemaking.

The word intimacy comes from the Latin intimatus. Intimatus means to make something known to someone. When you are intimate with someone, you are literally making yourself known to your partner. Every act of intimacy creates more intimacy. Each time you kiss, touch, make love you connect in an intimate way, you make yourself known. Get slack on intimate behaviour and you are no longer contributing to deeper intimacy. You then have to rely on the store of intimacy you have built up together. So continually share the intimate. It's the way to grow a deeper feeling of love.

The qualities for a successful sex life are the same ones that make for successful interpersonal relationships. Love. Commitment. Communication. A love relationship is an investment of emotions and time. When you put such serious life energy into the relationship, you want to feel that you are both going somewhere. Emotional continuity is vital for a long term relationship. Otherwise you'll constantly worry that the worst case scenario will happen. Your partner will walk out the door and out of your life. If you love each other with emotional consistency, you'll make a deeper commitment. Commitment to each other, creates true longevity for the relationship. Be emotionally reliable and put your energy into staying together. Strong relationships and dynamic sex needs commitment. Your relationship is strengthened when you have confidence that your relationship is secure. So in times of stress, you know you can rely on the security of your relationship to get you through.

Sex is emotionally healing. You feel happier, more generous, and trust yourself and others more. This happy feeling is easy to catch! People around you pick up on good moods. When you feel desired, wanted, loved, understood and sexually fulfilled, it shows.

Intimacy isn't just about doing things and going places together. Intimacy begins at the start of a relationship and grows over time depending on what you put into your relationship. So the more physically and emotionally true you both are, the more intimate you are. Intimacy is real. You can't pretend you have it. You can't fake it. You've got to make it.

LOVE AGENDAS

I LOVE YOU BECAUSE YOU'RE SEXY.

Let's look at the three most used words in the dictionary of lovers. I love you! It's easy to say. I love you. These words roll off your tongue. But notice how I love you, can come with certain conditions.

How about..."I love you, *because*." "I love you *because* you're strong." "I love you *because* you're attractive." "I love you *because* you're sexy"

Then there's the ..."I love you *if*." "I love you *if* you stay committed." "I love you *if* you give me what I want." "I love you *if* you're going to be rich."

This kind of love is love that must meet and maintain certain conditions. Love becomes restricted and constrained within boundaries. The danger of conditional love is this. When someone more attractive, or more successful turns up, the conditional lover is really impressed. When you base love on conditions, and those conditions change, you'll be back looking for more conditional love. Then another chapter begins in the never ending search for the perfect partner.

Partners who know they are loved for their strong points may be afraid to lose their looks or money or dance moves and spend all their time trying to keep up with expectations. They never let the partner see their vulnerable underbelly for fear of rejection. This lack of trust and inherent dishonesty affects the true potential of a loving relationship. In the reality of life, all things change, but true love is constant and unconditional.

SEX TALK

HONEST TALKING IS THE KEY TO GREAT SEX.

What you say and do at any time of the day affects your sex life. Talking together is essential for dynamic sex. Intensely intimate relationships happen when couples have great communication.

Blanshard & Blanshard know that the deepest need in a relationship is for closeness. Sharing part of yourself needs to be mutual. If you aren't communicating well, you'll notice that most things you talk about become issues. When your feelings and actions are misread, you think your partner should know you better. When this happens, there is no intimate talk about feelings. And the bottom line is no intimacy.

Responses are really important. Listening with empathy. Showing understanding. Giving feedback. Participating in the conversation. Let them know you recognise and understand what they are saying. Let them communicate hopes, dreams, ideas, fears, as well as everyday things. This gives them a feeling that they are heard and seen, which translates into a more positive attitude towards each other. If partners hold resentment and are having trouble communicating, then it shows up in your sex life. Many sexual issues can be resolved if sexual partners felt free to communicate openly.

Don't use the idea that one person can't fill all your needs to justify a lack of closeness in your relationship. You can improve intimacy between you out of the bedroom. Simply by treating each other like best friends. Because friends are genuinely interested in how you feel. Friends take turns talking and listening. When you speak and express opinions, friends don't get uncomfortable. They get interested, then make a point of getting involved in the subject, whatever the topic.

So pick up on the subjects your partner initiates. Break the habit of greeting a comment with silence. When they offer their point-of-view let them know it matters. Take what they say seriously. And show it by being supportive. When they forward ideas, be responsive. It works both ways. You validate your partner's opinions and give them personal credibility. And they do the same for you.

To find out what your partner thinks and how they are feeling you need to take time out to ask the question: How are you doing? Make a point to do it often. It's a way of saying I'm interested in what's going on with you. When you get to talking in a relaxed open way, like you do with a best friend, eighty-two percent of your relationship problems will be solved (or almost resolved). You'll have a great thing going for you, when you share an intellectual and emotional life together.

Do the intimate talk. Discuss things that your partner doesn't understand. Your relationship is too important to have misunderstandings between you. Exchange thoughts and ideas and immediately you'll feel closer to each other. And there's more to come. Great communication creates great intimacy.

You'll share more personal thoughts, personal feelings, ideas and future plans. Negative feelings will be replaced by positive ones. Once you define your emotional authenticity and share your interior life with your lover, you'll share greater intimacy. Instead of hiding your feelings to protect yourself, you'll both open up and expose yourselves. You'll talk together and not at each other.

Ask permission from each other to talk honestly and openly about your relationship. Then you can safely discuss issues you've been avoiding. There are no psychologists around here. Only you two know which issues you need to resolve to make your relationship work. You may have to admit you're wrong and that isn't easy. It's easier to find fault with your partner. No one is perfect and no one should point the finger. You know, you may be the one at fault.

Be honest. By being honest, you become more focused. Your discussions and problem solving capabilities as a couple improve dramatically. When this happens you begin to make positive changes and discover new ways to relate to each other. Both verbally and non-verbally.

MOOD

JAZZ UP YOUR LOVE LIFE.

Primitive body language is basic and can't be controlled or disguised.

When you know someone intimately, you are acutely aware of mood changes in their eyes, mouth and lips. The way someone looks at you. The body tells you exactly where it's at. Good moods can be deliciously contagious too. You want to share them. When you sense a sexy change in body code, you can't help it, you're genetically wired to jump in. But it's not in your best interest to get involved with a negative mood. Don't jump in if your partner is in a negative mood, because unfortunately it is also contagious. Contagious like flu. If you catch a bad mood then you're both down with it.

It's not up to you to change someone's negative mood. You're not an M.D. (*a Mood Doctor*) are you? You may see the subtle signs of emotional states. You may want to say the right thing to help the person along. But if either you or your partner doesn't want to have a conversation right at one particular moment, then leave it at that. People need to think things through, rather than thinking on their feet. Sleep on it. Write it out. It's important to figure out what is at the heart of the issue.

Taking time out to think about an issue, doesn't mean you don't want to discuss it later. Sometimes finding solutions takes time. It's up to a person to sort out their own stuff. Given time, they'll sort it out, without you! It's safe to let feelings run. Emotions are what make us human. As long as they aren't sweeping away the other partner in an emotional flood.

So, what about those who love languishing in long moods. Whether it is emotional or physical, we want to make things around us go well and it's not hard to pick up when our partner's feelings are out of whack. We can pick up on these feelings that hang in the atmosphere. Long moody episodes create emotional pollution. Unvoiced negative moods get heavy and dark. They create an invisible disturbance around the place. One partner is left guessing why the other is acting like this. And no matter how hard they try to shake the happy rattle...the mood is unsmiling. This leaves the other one wondering, why? Is it me? Are they mad at me? What have I done? You rewind the days conversations trying to figure out this pervading moodiness.

Partners want more jazz in their life. That's why constant moody blues sessions erode the intimate bond necessary for a long term loving relationship. If you're in a regular bad mood, take note. Accept the fact that you do need to discuss what is going on.

Some partners are masters of the long sulk. They make a conscious decision to use a long moody sulk to force an issue. These moods are weapons to get what they want; such as the latest mobile phone or sex or more attention. They withdraw into monosyllables and turn the relationship into a strategy game. It's all so tedious. And they know it! That's the point.

Moods show and everyone can see them. You've heard that expression, 'She's such a moody person'. 'He's always packing a sad'. Constant moodiness starts to look like your personality trait. No one can satisfy you. You become known as a person with a personality problem. Eventually your partner loses respect and closes off emotionally and physically because you are too difficult to live with.

However you don't have to be preoccupied with the emotional status of your partner. That's exhausting. Give each other space. Then instead of playing moody blues, you can play up with each other.

EMOTIONAL LIBRARY

MAKE ROOM FOR A NEW LOVE STORY.

In every relationship, you have experiences, good and bad. All of these personal experiences are stored in the vault of yourself. Some people call it emotional baggage. *Blanshard & Blanshard* prefer to call it the Emotional Library. In these relationship archives, every experience, every reflection, every argument, every joke, becomes a catalogue, defined and cross-referenced to other relationships. When you come face to face with a difficult situation, it's easy to pull down a chapter of experiences from another relationship. Some days you can find yourself dragging out old memories of your past relationships. It's so easy to overlay your previous responses onto current situations And it's so wrong. When you filter everything through your catalogue of past experiences, you're not connecting up in a fresh new way as a couple.

New experiences challenge us every day. Which means we are constantly developing and changing as people. And we need to embrace this. Change renews us. In fact, every seven years our bones, muscles and tissues renew themselves. So does our heart. Love is also a renewable resource, but you've got to work at it.

Change is also part of moving on in any relationship. Part of moving on is about leaving things behind. Especially previous lovers. Yet, some people inadvertently or blatantly invite their past lovers back into their lives. By talking them up or down to the new lover, they compare old loves with new loves. And they use social symbols to do it. How strong, how sexy, how rich, how handsome, how beautiful, how talented.

If you have a habit of talking about your previous partners, what are you really doing? Are you subconsciously trying to shape your present partner into the best of your past lovers? Is this what you want? How does your present partner feel about that?

The same goes for arguments. If you've argued about something and sorted it, try to let it go and not bring the same issue up again. Don't bring an old disagreement into your current one. See your partner as they are right now. Keep the past in the past. If you're committed to having a long term relationship make a decision to shelve previous arguments and relationships. This makes room for a whole new love story. The relationship script is being written all the time.

TALK THE TALK

DO YOU DO ALL THE TALKING.

Do you do all the talking? Telling your partner how it is, from the minute they wake up. Over espresso, over toast, over eggs. Over and over. Till the light goes out. Some people announce every little thing they are thinking. And talk about everything they're going to do or not do. When their news is switched on all day, you switch off. Right?

Listening to continual information makes it difficult to differentiate verbal chatter from the need to engage in important discussions. A busy mind filled with monkey chatter leaves no space for exchanging meaningful ideas and thoughts. So if you want to hear what your partner thinks, stop talking. Don't announce every little thing you're going to do.

Make your bed a discussion-free zone. There's no room for words & dossiers between the sheets. We're talking about body language only. It's important to keep your bedroom life private. Do you talk to your friends about your relationship? Do you discuss intimate details about your love life with your family, your therapist or confide in someone you just met? When you discuss intimate details, it's like having someone else in bed with you two.

Here's the drill. For every sentence you tell your Mother or your best friend, make sure your lover gets the full paragraph. After all, your partner is your confidant and they should know how you're feeling, and what's going on way before anyone else does. It's about relationship confidentiality.

Relationship confidential means there are secrets you don't share with the rest of the world. That's how you keep your relationship intimate. You keep confidences, secrets, all that beautiful intimacy between you and your lover belongs exclusively to you as a couple.

THE BIG V

THE LOUDER YOU TALK
THE LESS YOU THINK.

Can you be loud enough to overpower the voice of someone who interrupts or contradicts you. Going beyond the pitch of your voice and increasing the volume drowns out all reason. While you are shouting, you can't figure out the arguments, because the louder you shout the less you think. That's a scientific fact. Getting mad doesn't get you anywhere. You may shout until the early hours of the morning and problems are still not resolved. Problems seem worse than when you started. Do you think shouting is the only way to let someone know how bad you feel. It's the opposite. Shouting makes your partner feel bad.

Damage from arguments happens when one or both of you are shouting. As soon as you shout, the discussion or disagreement gets upgraded to a fight. You are not looking to reason and sort things out. You can't because you are shouting. Resentment and bad feelings held by one or both of you, continue this way. Once you lower your voices and both start talking you stop the ongoing collateral damage.

Never yell at each other. Don't raise your voice. Ever. By not raising your voices during an argument you have the best chance of resolving any issue between you. And maintain a tone of respect and love, even when saying hard things to each other.

AMNESIA

"YOU NEVER TOLD ME THAT."

Does your partner appear to have selective amnesia? You tell them something important and a few days later they say, you never told me that. They only hear what they want. They don't remember what you said.

How can you understand your partner, the heart pouring itself out to you, if you half listen to what they are saying and feeling. Not being able to talk about feelings, makes a person feel lonely. Just because you are with someone, you may not be reaching each other. So you may both be living emotionally alone.

The loneliness comes from knowing you can't contact another person's feelings, no matter how hard you try. You can be living with someone, but not be really sharing a life. It's true. Anyone can be lonely in love.

If you don't think you're being heard, what can you do? Try rephrasing what you've just said. Effective communication is not just saying things, but having things heard. Don't wait for your partner to initiate deep talks. You need to get their full attention. Don't try to talk about important issues while they are distracted or you're both busy. Tell them there is something you need to talk about. Can I talk to you about... (be specific here) ? Wait for them to answer. If they say no, then say we need to make a time. Book the space. See yourself as relationship executives and manage your interpersonal time. No one else can sort it for you. It's your private business.

Keep in mind, physical and emotional bonds are nurtured through attentive, effective communication. Communication is the glue that bonds your relationship together. Without this kind of foreplay, things get really screwed up. So each partner must take responsibility to get the listening part right. How can you improve your relationship communication skills? Take time out over coffee, put down the magazine, mute the remote. Make space to communicate. Talk about your future dreams together. It's a chance to open yourself up and allow another to see your ideas, thoughts and emotions. This strengthens and deepens the love between you.

RELATIONSHIP
TAI CHI

CREATING A BALANCED
EQUAL RELATIONSHIP.

All intimate relationships are about energy. Energy shared. Energy taken. Energy given away and power unrecognised. In the context of a relationship, conversations and body language between partners make a dialogue that determines the balance of power. Often one person in the relationship dominates; by being more determined; by using a stronger more distinctive voice; by having the first and last say.

Having to negotiate every situation with a power play partner is exhausting. If one person is dominating, they may be equating intimacy with a form of license to be the star. In this case there may as well be only one person in the relationship. The Star. It's all about them in their stellar role. This is not what should happen in a shared relationship. If this is happening, you'll have one thing going. Big, fat, ugly resentment.

When there is a main star in a relationship, the focus is on them and what their personal needs are. They feel they are always right and their partner is mostly wrong. The star likes to do things their way.

This imbalance becomes visible and shows up as someone who has the last say, someone who is teasing is not listening. Someone who doesn't want to understand. Someone who makes you feel dis-empowered. Someone who always pushes your buttons.

Imbalances in relationships happen when one of the partners doesn't care how they are affecting the other person. You can be in love with someone but not show care for them. You don't look at their needs or listen to them. What they say doesn't matter as much as what you say. What they want doesn't matter as much as what you want. So even if they say that something bothers them, you pay little attention. This is emotional strong arming. Instead of two-way communication, it's one way. Your way.

It's too easy to do things your own way. Thinking you're loving someone and doing everything your own way, is not caring about someone else. You do things for them. Sure, you buy flowers, but the ones you like. You watch TV with them, but you hold the remote. You supermarket shop, but buy what you like, you make dinner, but only cook what you like to eat. You would never dream of ironing a shirt for them, never load the washing machine with their things. You don't bother changing the sheets or towels. You rely on them to do all that. Put your feet up and watch TV, now that's more like it.

To care about somebody else you have to listen to their needs, what they like, what they want to do. So if you're the star in your relationship, you could find yourself left alone in your own empty universe. Reflect on how you currently do things. Are you the star in your relationship? Take a look. The star takes 'The Starring Role'. The star always thinks they have a faster, better answer to all situations and takes on the responsibility to ensure their brilliant idea is followed through. Is your pure brilliance the right way to do things? Not necessarily. The know it all attitude, acting arrogant, negating, or looking for a way to one-up whatever a partner says, can become a habit. The star has answers to questions you didn't even ask. Telling you what to do and how to do it.

And isn't it amazing, when you are on your own how you manage to be in control, stay in control and survive, without helpful suggestions! The back seat driver is a classic star scenario. It's often a cause for arguments and embarrassing flare-ups in public. Dramatic outcomes for ordinary moments, like parking the car. When the star runs interference in public spaces there's a battle for power, which looks crazy but is entertaining for onlookers. Then the argument is dragged home, like pugilistic takeaways, to be fought out, for hours later. It makes doing things together tense and less fun. Pretty soon you start making excuses to leave one or other at home.

Intervening while someone is trying to negotiate a situation, creates confusion and frustration. The partner who's trying to sort things, doesn't need quips, interjections, or smart answers from the star.

So if you're the one that's kibitzing, take your

hands off the controls. Butt-out. Resist looking over your partners collarbone. Stop with the comments. Give the respect you expect to get. Don't tell your partner what to do or how to do it. Let your partner finish what they've started. When someone is in control of a situation, let them finish whatever they are doing, without unasked for verbal assistance. Let them drive the car, find a car park, book the hotel, choose the wine and complain about the food. The way you do something is often totally different to how they do it. Give your partner space to do things their way. And look forward to holding hands in public again.

Power and control versus emotional withholding. Both are power plays. There are no winners. There are only Lovers who need to share ideas and decide things together without pressure and conflict. You both walk the planet in your own way and you're both brilliant. So when your partner explains something to you, try to understand why they feel or think that way.

When you develop qualities of openness and support, you share a developed inner emotional world with your partner. Creating a balanced and equal relationship is far more rewarding than winning. Find out how your partner thinks and feels. Respect how your partner thinks and feels. Equality strengthens your partnership.

WEWE

TWO INDIVIDUALS, LIVING DYNAMICALLY TOGETHER.

You can be so into each other that you can blend yourselves into one homogeneous couple. We think. We eat. We go. We drink. We have. We drive. We like. You become mirrors of each other instead of maintaining your essential nature as individuals. You love each other too much. You start to think alike, act the same and do everything with the other you.

Then you feel the need to change things. You start a pattern of trying to change each other to make a better "you & me". This is one of the worst things you can do in a relationship. You simply forget who you are in relation to each other. So many things make-up who you are as an individual. Your choices, your friends, your tastes, and your quirky habits.

Blanshard & Blanshard have proved that a relationship can grow and develop far beyond ordinary possibilities. To make this happen, you need to do two things.

First, be yourself by making a point of maintaining your own idiosyncrasy. Your rarity, passion, monomania, mannerisms and obsessions, make you who you are. How you do things is unique and part of your identity. How you look, think, act, or what you say, makes a unique individual. Be who you are. Keep your own quirky habits. Be more of who you are not less of yourself. It gives you self-esteem. A full quota of self-esteem is empowering. You'll drive your own destiny. And encompass others, including your lover.

Second, open your eyes and take a closer look at that special individual you fell in love with. Because they are who they are. And you are you. Simple as that. If you must change someone, then look in the mirror Give your partner room to become more of who they are, not less than themselves. That way, a fruity complexity develops in your relationship.

As strong individuals you make a formidable team. Whether it's a new baby, a new job, winning a lottery or losing your financial empire. When two lovers realize their full potential as individuals, your partnership is double espresso to go. It gives you power to adapt to any social physical or emotional dynamic in life.

NANU

MASTER YOUR OWN UNIVERSE.

There are moments when you have a gut feeling to do something, like phoning a friend. And as soon as, you hear their voice, you know in one nanu second the reason you called. But, how hard is it to act on spontaneous feelings, when your partner interjects with helpful, useful, thoughtful, better suggestions. When someone interferes and suggests alternatives, they inadvertently stop you making your connection. You don't go ahead and do what you felt you needed to do. That split second in time, which reveals something just for you, vanishes.

Rare moments in life get missed when you don't follow up on your intuition. Let personal spontaneity into your life. That way you can master your own universe and share your discoverics. Respect and Respond to intuition. Give each other plenty of R & R.

PEEL YOUR OWN BANANA

MAKE YOUR LOVE LIFE FRUITY.

When someone has a plan, watch you don't smother it with alternative suggestions. If someone comes up with an idea first, go with it. This means, if it's red curry at Little India, don't suggest pepperoni pizza at Gino's. Learn to accept other people's ideas. Try not to adapt or alter their ideas and substitute yours. Enjoy the fruits of their thoughts. Self awareness, humility and respect are important in relationships.

The qualities you bring to your relationship are like a gift. The more you give, the more the relationship works. The more you both give, the more likely the relationship will grow, and the sexual passion and intimacy you share becomes unlimited. We often restrict ourselves, we hold back from giving as much as we could. Sex, love, passion and intimacy respond to the amount of effort you give out.

Let's face it. When you met you were total strangers. And you gave each other everything. This was your bond. Then you got to know each other intimately. Now you can see the outline of each other's smile with your eyes closed. When you know someone intimately, you're in sync. You seem to know what the other is going to say, before they've said it. You find yourselves finishing each others sentences. At times it's seamless, as if you've got the same heart beat. Then one partner starts to think their way is better. They like to re-vamp your ideas. When you suggest an idea, they put forward another. No matter what you suggest, they have another suggestion, until you can't be bothered thinking about it. If someone always has the last say, the oneness becomes numbness.

If you don't value what your partner thinks, their energy will go and they'll go cold on you. And how an idea is put forward is important. When you have a thought, don't present it as a question. Should we? Can we? Do you think? How about? What do you think? Forget these continuous questions. When you put forward a good idea as a question, you're asking someone to judge it. So expect to have your idea critiqued and possibly have your mind changed. You don't think or act the same as your partner. You never will! That's great. Life is incredibly interesting together. Life can be unique, when you make it that way. The voyage of the best relationship is a zig zag line of a hundred ideas and they're not all yours. So don't run a straight line through life together, zig zag. Relationships are about give and take not give give or take take.

THE SPECIALISTS

STIMULATE
YOUR RELATIONSHIP I.Q.

Ever notice in relationships how one partner becomes the sleeper. The other becomes the expert. Like a specialist in the relationship, the expert is always asked about specific things. They become the maitre de, the epicurean authority, the horticulturist with the green thumb, the mechanic and tyre repair specialist. One partner relies on the other's expertise. They often ask questions like: what do you want to eat? What shall we buy? How does this work? Can you fix this? While it sounds like a practical idea, *Blanshard & Blanshard* believe it turns the relationship into a sleepy backwater.

Now imagine having two individuals in the relationship who both know how things work. You both understand widgets. Organic composting. Four green hands instead of one green thumb. Your ordinary kitchen becomes a gourmet kitchen with two great chefs sautéing different dishes. Swap recipes for jumbo shrimp or gazpacho and you'll have a more dynamic scenario.

Do research; gain knowledge and make decisions. Use your creative juices. Share your ideas. Stimulating the senses makes you more intelligent. Even if you don't notice a change in I.Q. quota, you'll definitely have a great time admiring each others bonsai and eating each others goulash. Extend your abilities. Make individual decisions. Stimulate your relationship I.Q.

VOLCANO

ARE YOU LIVING WITH A STINKER?

Imagine continuing to live with someone who thinks nothing of dropping a sulphur bomb in the bed and laughing about it. Funny thing is, it's not funny. Someone who takes control of the TV remote, drops clothes, leaves dishes. Don't you hate annoying habits. So why do they insist on doing them?

Annoying habits are like an argument in mime. All action and no words. Then, if anyone does complain, they are accused of nagging! So what is really going on?

If objectionable habits continue, even after you have highlighted them, there is an underlying problem. Disguised as humourous antidotes or forgetfulness, annoying habits are used for power-playing the relationship. Power-plays cause unspoken resentment. Eventually a partner stops nagging and the Annoyer thinks they are getting away with their actions. Not necessarily. For every action there is a reaction. The Annoyer forgets that someone has a tipping point. A point when the person living with them gets totally fed up with power play games. And then they withhold other things in the relationship to counter the power play. So if you're full of yourself, all gas and hot air, you'll get nowhere in the bedroom. Clean up your act and get more action.

THE LAWS OF DESIRE

WE NEVER HAVE SEX ANY MORE!

Ask someone who has been in a relationship for a while and you'll hear the same complaint. They never get enough sex any more. That's the biggest moan from men and woman. He/she just isn't interested. They all say it's the partners fault.

Blanshard & Blanshard believe, if you want to be sexy, you've got to feel sexy. It's all up to you! How you feel about yourself translates into the physical.

Look after your general health and well-being with diet and exercise. Take care of your physical appearance. Also no one wants to go to bed with someone whose body odor reminds them of hamburgers, or whose breath has run out of mouthwash. It's sexual physics.

There is a way of up-scaling the way you look. Remember when you were dating. You made an effort to look more attractive. So why stop now! Have a date night every week. Why not every night.

How can you vamp things up? You can buy new soap, aftershave, underwear, perfume, throw out the well trodden socks. Buy brand new lingerie. Replace the tired and exhausted, unlovable lace for cottons, satins and silk.

Enroll in the gym again. Why not sign up and take some classes together! Rev up the endorphins. That way and you'll keep up the sweaty, sexy stuff.

Here's the list to get physical: Improved diet and supplements. You are what you eat! Gym. Fresh air. Sunshine. Showers. Kissable breath. A non smoker's breath. Annual health checks with dentist and doctor. Maintain a healthy weight. Look in the mirror and check out the clothes you wear around your partner. Are you attracted to what you see? Relaxed casual does not mean slacking off and going into slob mode disguised as shabby chic!

And here's another thing, do you ask your partner, how does this look? What do you think of my... (insert any anatomical part in this space)? Take care of yourself. Your partner is not your oral hygienist, dresser, make-up or make-over artist. If you invite your partner to keep an eye on your physical appearance, they'll develop a seriously bad habit of constantly checking you out. They'll be in your face 24/7 because you asked them to be your personal assistant. If you slide under their microscope, you make yourself available for observation. You allow them to become your body critic and before you know it they're making comments like: you're getting a bit fat, just thought you should know; you should grow your fingernails so your stubby fingers look longer. Don't ask your partner to be your talking mirror. Look out for yourself and they'll be on the lookout for you!

LOVE ON TOP

THE MISSIONARY OF LOVE.

If you get too preoccupied to put lovemaking at the top of your list, take a look at what's going on. Are you facing more personal demands that impact on time you have together. Has your workload increased. Do you have more bills to pay. The good news is this. As long as you have time to spend the night in bed together, you can get the sex back together too.

O.K, so let's say you are believers in each other and your relationship. That is a great start. To bring sex back into focus, try this; make a soft rule where you each get one night a week to say no thank you to having sex (for whatever reason you think of). Then add in another soft option; as a couple you can agree on a non-sex night. So two nights of no sex. Agreed. You get both nights off if you're tired or had an exhausting day. Now you're thinking how does having no sex increase your desire for each other.

You've both guaranteed sex four nights a week if you want! You can talk about ways to make those four days sexually orientated, such as showering together, having massages and whatever intimate things you love.

There is time in the day to keep your sex life together. And you need to make the most of those moments. Saying goodbye with a kiss. Hug and kiss each other every chance you get. Hormones in your saliva are biological ways nature has of keeping you connected. Kissing keeps you connected. Make a point of connecting with your lover each day, no mater what is going on in your world.

Agree on a time every evening when you both stop your day. You can turn down the lights, light candles, play music. You are not trying to create a mood by faking a romantic moment. You are just being together in the moment. You keep the sexual vibes going. Practise keeping the world out for a moment. The job, business, kids, friends and family. Responsibilities, commitments and routine can impact negatively on your sex drive and intimacy. So take time to switch off the day and tune into each other. Avoid talking about problems for a while. Drink the wine and let the world be the world.

SEXUAL SAFARI

ANIMALS
IN FANCY SHOES.

An active sex life is an important part of any great relationship. If your bedroom is boring there's a world of other places that can revitalise your sex life. It's up to you!

As long as you don't make yourselves a public nuisance, sex doesn't necessarily have to be restricted to the bedroom. Common sense rules! If you're worried about decency laws or sight-seers, make love in your car down by the wharf in the moonlight, or park up on lovers' leap, where you can be seen and heard!

Cars, trains, planes. Wild and creative things you do together, create a bonding experience. Sneaky sex in public places is illegal of course. People do it, but you may prefer to follow social rules. Or if you do take a calculated risk, you could find the whole thing exciting...until you both get caught butt-naked!

Vigorous exercise or massive excitement activates

the sympathetic nervous system. After exercise you are more quickly aroused. Physically challenging activities get your brain geared up for sex. They drive up the action of dopamine, the neurotransmitter that gives a feeling of satisfaction and pleasure and pumps up testosterone.

So do something neither of you have done before. Something physical, like taking up scuba diving, snowboarding, or a martial arts class! Excitation transfer happens when you do challenging things together. And even when you are couch buddies watching scary movies, you can get a full adrenalin surge and jump into each others arms. All your senses are fired up. When you're hot you also transfer energy and excitement to each other. Jump up and down or jump into bed!

SEXUAL APPETITE

HUNGRY FOR MORE SEX.

When you have sex you use up certain vitamins and minerals, especially zinc. But if you don't replace zinc, your body runs on empty. You'll find yourself lacking your usual sexual drive.

Zinc can be replaced by taking vitamin supplements. Or by a trip to your local fish market. Shuck an oyster and you're looking at a storehouse of natural zinc. Oysters are the number one food for sex. Zinc brings the X back to sex. Zinc produces testosterone. Zinc is important for men and women. Having sex, drinking coffee, caffeine beverages, drinking alcohol or smoking are all things that increase your need for zinc. The more zinc you have, the more you are into having sex.

Other foods super rich in zinc are lean red meat, fish and shellfish, chicken, egg yolk, brown, yellow and green lentils, brown rice and green leafy vegetables.

Soy is another sex food. Double your order of soy

beans when you're eating sushi. Those green soy beans are power packed for sexual health. Soy beans, tofu and soy milk are also excellent low fat proteins, which contain phytoestrogens. Two servings of soy can prevent symptoms of premenstrual syndrome. Phytoestrogens regulate hormones and prevent mood swings and food cravings. Soy binds to estrogen receptors. Drinking soy products or eating soy daily, helps to keep a woman's vagina lubricated. That's a nice touch! Soy helps men have a healthy prostate. The prostate is an essential organ for sex, so keep it healthy.

Put more capsaicin, in your diet. Capsaicin gives green and red chilies their fire! Red hot chili peppers are spicy stimulus for hot sex!

Your heart affects your sexual health because it pumps blood through your body. In men blood pumps into the penis = erection. Way to go! You've heard that lean meat, chicken and fish are best for heart health. So it makes sense to cut off all visible fat and skin when preparing meat and poultry. Steam, broil and boil. Bypass the deep fryer. Your heart and arteries won't appreciate deep fried fish and chips like you do. Make a conscious decision to refuse fast foods, like mega-pizza, hamburgers and fried chicken. Avoid any foods that could compromise sexual performance. Love your food. Stay sex-hungry.

HOME SEX

SEXUAL RENOVATIONS.

A sensual environment is essential to your sex life. It's easy to create a home environment that stimulates your five senses. To see, smell, hear, touch and taste. First, take a look around your house or apartment. Go from room to room and see if the rooms you spend time together have a sensual quality or not. Can you see, smell, touch, taste, and hear a myriad of sensual things there?

Check out the bedroom. Sexy or boring? The color of the curtains or blinds, the color on the walls. The sheets and pillows. Is the room thrown together with accumulated bits and pieces or is the environment sensual. By the colors on the walls and fabrics on the bed, fresh cut flowers, exotic fragrances, glowing candles and essential oils burning, you can create a sexual space that arouses the senses.

When you create a sensual and sacred environment, you make a special place where you're not distracted or interrupted. A room like this is essential for lovemaking. Every couple needs this kind of space. Consciously create a sensuous environment so everything you do there is focused: making love, massaging, lying in candlelight listening to music, watching sexy, romantic, or erotic movies. Do anything and everything you two love doing together, in the privacy of your own home.

BOOKS BY BEST SELLING AUTHORS
BLANSHARD & BLANSHARD

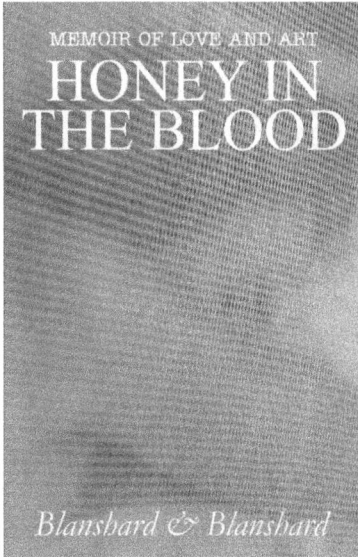

MEMOIR OF LOVE AND ART
HONEY IN THE BLOOD

Blanshard & Blanshard

ISBN 978-0-9807155-7-6

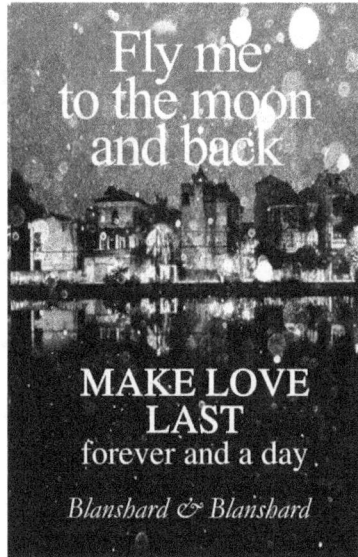

Fly me to the moon and back

MAKE LOVE LAST
forever and a day

Blanshard & Blanshard

ISBN 978-0-9807155-0-7

HOW TO MAKE LOVE LAST
KEEP THE SEX DIRTY & THE FIGHTS CLEAN

Blanshard & Blanshard

ISBN 978-0-9807155-3-8

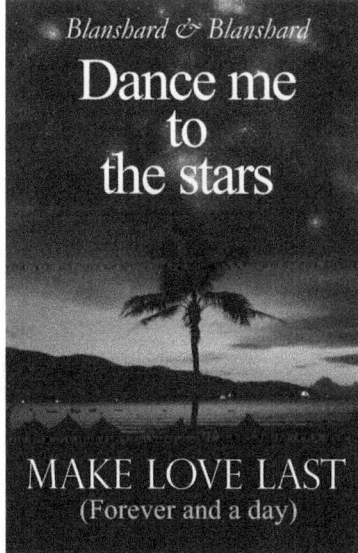

Blanshard & Blanshard
Dance me to the stars

MAKE LOVE LAST
(Forever and a day)

ISBN 978-0-9807155-8-3

www.ingramcontent.com/pod-product-compliance
Lightning Source LLC
Chambersburg PA
CBHW052216270326
41931CB00011B/2371